ONE MAN'S MIND
A COLLECTION OF POEMS

JOHN MASK

One Man's Mind
ISBN 978-0-9818956-3-5
Copyright 2009 John Mask
Request for information should be addressed to:
Curry Brothers Marketing and Publishing Group
P.O. Box 62314
Colorado Springs, CO 80962
cbmpg@yahoo.com

All rights reserved. No part of this publication may be reproduced, stored in a retrieval system, or transmitted in any form or by any means, electronic, mechanical, photocopy, recording, or any other, except for brief quotations in printed reviews, without the prior permission of the publisher.

CURRY BROTHERS MARKETING
AND PUBLISHING GROUP

Dedications

I thank God for the strength and for the ability to write this book. Most of all, it is my prayer that you the reader might read something in this book that will change your thoughts, your insights, or life as a whole. I pray that I have said something that has touched your lives, like never before. There are several individuals and groups of people who have played a tremendous role in my life and I would be remised if I did not mention a few of them. Naturally, there is not enough time or space to recognize everyone who has played a tremendous part in saving my soul, and teaching me about life. For those that I overlook, please charge it to my head and not my heart, because there are several angles I have known along life's journey that have raised me from the depths of my personal pitfalls. First, I would like to thank God who is the head of my life, my mother Darlene Nelson, my daddy Floyd Mask Sr., my siblings Phyllis Greer, Regina Mask, Wendy Turner, Sone Redmon, Barbara Glenn, Floyd Mask Jr., Geneva Mask, Donald Mask, Charles Baker, Stayce Walker, my Pastor Gerald Coleman and all the members of Faith-Keepers Ministries in Memphis, Tennessee and my children Marquita, Joshua, and Ashante. I would like to give a very special dedication to the people who encouraged me to be what God has set for me to see this dream come true. They are Kenneth Harbert, Simone Hodge, Crystal Butler, Harold Watson Jr., Pholesha Middlebrooks, Alberta A.Sanders, Rody Walker, Marvin Sangster, and David Jackson. I would also like to recognize the people who play a very special part in my daily life, Deborah Scott, Dee Daniels, Fameka Lee, the Concentra Medical Staff, my Metro Foods Family, Securtas and its wonderful employees, Faith Jones, Ms. Boone, Tina Isha, Jamie Collier, the Liggins family, Sgt. Askew, Ms. Ford and her fantastic ministry. Also, thank you to those that are no longer here with us, but have played a tremendous role in my life and personal development, James Jelks, Clarence Palmer (Cold Crush Brothers), John Hubbard, Glenn Currie, and Sherry King. You may be gone, but never forgotten! Thank you again for taking the time to pick up this book and again I pray that it can be as much a blessing to you, the reader, as it has been for me in taking thetime to write it.

God Bless!
John Mask

Contents

                                                                    Page
Black Woman 4
Intimacy 5
I Hear The Screams, Do You Know What I Mean 6
Can I Love You? 8
My Flower. 9
Fill My Cup 10
Men 11
Missing You 12
You're Gone 13
Hurt 14
Can We Talk 15
Hold Your Man 16
The Hood 17
How I Love You 18
What Do You Want From Me? 19
Lead Me 20
2—Faced 21
You Are The One For Me 22
Choices 23
My Heart Cries 24
My Friend 25
Only God Knows 26
Heartbreak 27
Springtime 28
Thirsty 29
Touch Me 30
Knowledge 31
Why Do You? 32
Eavesdropping 33
Stop 34
Good Bye 35
Forever 36
24 37
Yes, Lord 38
Blood, Sweat and Tears 39
Mother 40

Black Woman

Black woman, when you look in the mirror what do you see?
Are you looking at past hurts or do you see victory?
When you look in my eyes, what do you see?
A future or a lone night stand that could be?
Black woman, why do you get mad when I grab a white hand
When you're supposed to be my black Queen
from the mother land?
A strong, beautiful, black woman, different than any kind
Not a woman that attracts a man by shaking her behind.
Black woman, black woman where did we go wrong
When you used to be so confident, supportive and strong?
Now, I see a fragment of what used to be
Black Queen taking off her crown and that's killing me.
Disrespecting their kings, bringing in all types of drama
Trying to raise a king, "Hey! You ain't his mama".
Here I come, your black king. Let me take you by your hand
Dust you off, clean you up (here's your crown)
And take you back to the mother land.
Not to kill you but to instill in you the plan that God has
For your black man.
To love you, to hold you, to walk hand in hand
When you go to church listening to the preacher man,
To share in our possession that God has blessed
You hear me black queen, "I don't want no mess".
So, here I am letting go of the white and taking your hand.
Thank you my black woman, for making me a black man.

Intimacy

Intimacy is not what comes out of me
or something I put into thee.
Something we share when we look into each other's eyes
Not when a man is rubbing between a woman's thighs.
Intimacy is more than rubbing, kissing and making them
Feel right
And definitely more than spending a night.
Intimacy is you being there for one another,
Being there regardless, and forsaking all others.
Intimacy is not when you see me; you want to go to bed
If that's all you want, then what's going on in your head?
Can you hold me, and not scold me?
Can you pick me up when I am torn down?
Taking away the disappointment, and turning them around
Can you love me for me and not for something you see,
When I'm sick, can you nurse me back to health?
Can you put me back right when I go left?
Can you hold me? Love me when I'm old and gray,
Especially if I can't perform on that special day?
Can you love me for me? If you can, that's the
beginning of
Intimacy.

I Hear the Screams, Do you Know what I Mean?

Please, please help me to understand, why would you allow a man
To beat you, cheat you, to use you and abuse you.
You go to work every day, trying to pave a better way
For your kids to stay in a better place
I hear the screams, do you know what I mean?
A man that you want to be his wife
But when you come home, he's cussing, fussing and threatening
You with a knife
He's out late at night, and you're holding your kids tight
Praying to God that all this will go away
But it starts back up again the next day
He kicks you, beats you, until you almost passed out.
You say, "I'm not going to work today", but you hear a voice
Saying, "You better get the hell out".
You go to work late with a black eye, people are staring
And wondering why
This woman has shades on and it's raining outside.
When you open your mouth, then the lies fly.
You try to justify all the wrong
A woman sits in a corner shaking her head saying,
"Different day, but the same song".
I hear the screams, do you know what I mean?
A couple of years later, through all the prayers and all the cries,
The man finally dies.
You're thinking 'I'll finally get some peace now that he's deceased'
Then you realized, that you're contemplating suicide.
"Now that he's gone, how can I carry on?"

Saying to yourself, "Yes I can be strong".
Until a man comes into your life and wants to make you his wife
"Why don't you just walk away? It's not that easy", I say
Inside my mind he's still teasing me; in my spirit he's still beating me
Now do you hear my screams, do you know what I mean?

Can I love you?

Can I love you? It's not something you just say,
It's how you expressed it each and every day
Walking from place to place, holding hand in hand
Not to make anyone jealous, just letting people know
That you are my woman and yes, I am your man
Buying you roses, not because I did any wrong
But you picked me up when I was hurting and not so strong
I'll like to touch you in places, which you haven't been touched
In awhile,
Not to get you excited, but to see you smile
To hold you, rub you all through the night
Kissing you 'til the feeling becomes so, so right
Women say, "It's hard for a man to love a woman",
I don't understand?
Relax!
So let me sit back, think for a moment
And take you to love land.
Can I love you?

My Flower

My delicate, yet precious flower
Yet, I'll never ever try to devour
You, nor will I mistreat or abuse you.
You're special to me like I'm special to you.
I'll water you and nourish you each and every day.
When I talk to you, it will be in our own special way.
Early in the morning,
I'll take you out so that everyone could see
That my flower is very dear to me.
When the sun goes down, the day turns into night
I'll bring you back into the house
So no one can steal your spotlight.
Precious you are to me in every way,
When I found you I didn't care what people had to say,
You were not that pretty, that you were no good
I stopped listening to all the negative words
And brought you to another neighborhood.
Now, I see what real beauty is to me
A little sun, a little fun
Some positive words can go a long way,
I see the results (beauty) that's expressed on your face.
My time with you is not that long
That's why I sat down and expressed my feelings for you
While writing this poem.

Fill My Cup

When I'm at home and all alone
And there's no one I can call on the phone
Can you fill my cup?
There's no noise in my house
I'm quieter than a church mouse
No one to talk to; I have nothing else to do
Can you fill my cup?
In my mind I can't go any higher,
But you promised to give me my heart's desire
Can you fill my cup?
When I fall and hit the floor,
Deep down in my heart I can't take it anymore
Can you fill my cup?
When it's dark outside and I can't find my way
Can you take me by the hand and lead the way
When someone dear to me dies and tears are
Rolling down my eyes
Tell me, "Can you feel my cup"?

Men

Why do you say all men are dogs?
Have you met every man?
Have you owned every dog?
God has put various men into your life
That doesn't mean that every man wants you to
Be his wife.
Just look at the men that you meet
You love them, hate them, and you hurt
But you have to take the bitter with the sweet
Be careful of the men that you date; marry
Your relationship could be abusive, stressful
Fatal that that's scary
Just take a moment to look at the choices you make
Sorry, it may already be too late.

Missing You

Sitting in my room, racking my brains
But the truth of the matter; it still remains
Are the memories of me and you?
And how my heart misses a beat being without you.
Playing the radio, listening to our favorite song
(the lyrics are too emotional, heartfelt and long)
Just thinking about our past
And how we couldn't make our relationship last
Remembering all the fun we shared,
And how the sun glared
At that beautiful smile that last from miles and miles
We would sit in front of the fireplace
We were hand-in-hand, face to face
Talking and holding each other all through the night
Seeing who would stay up the longest
Before we turned off the lights
I still don't know what to do
Deep down my heart's still missing you.
Missing you is a very hard thing
When you used to come by, cooked me dinner
And all the joy you used to bring
I thank God everyday that you came my way
I hope this poem finds you, and you can say
I miss you too.

You're Gone

Missing you and not realizing that you're gone
It's hard to come to the conclusion that life has to go on
To miss someone that has been special in your life
Regardless of if it were a girlfriend, a good friend, boyfriend
Husband and/or wife
To finally realize they're no longer around
Could make you upset, depressed and try to bring you down
Looking at the pictures, remembering all the fun
Thinking about all those stupid arguments
And realizing they were really dumb
If only I could turn back the hands of time
Or at least hold you one more time
I would give you a very long kiss
Then let you know that deep down in my heart
You are truly missed.

Hurt

There are two types of hurt; you hurt someone
Or they hurt you
There are various ways of how people get hurt
Hurt by a loved one, on the job, even in the church
There are several ways how you can deal with the
Hurt
You can play like you don't care
Play it off or just let it hurt
You can try it your way, then there's God's way
The Lord says, "Cast your cares upon me, 'cause I care for you".
Also, "all those that labor and have heavy labors
Come upon me and I will give you rest".
So the next time you hurt and going through
Lean on Jesus; He'll pull you through.

Can We Talk

Before we begin to talk, can we enjoy a long walk?
On the beach; where I can massage your feet
And feed you something sweet to eat
Come, sit down beside me so we can communicate
Before this night is over, you'll be my soul mate
Sit right there so I can look into your eyes
Something looks funny, o' now I realize
I see all the hurt you've been going through
Don't worry about it; I've been down that same road
Excuse me, I'm not here to talk about your past
I just want to hold you, talk to you and try
To make this night last
You know I've been trying to talk to you for a while
You're such a beautiful person and I love your smile
So, come here, let me hold you for our last moments
That's how I would like our last minutes spent
I realized it's getting late, but could tell me
Did you enjoy our date?
How about we see each other tomorrow
Same place, time around 8?

Hold Your Man

Ladies, hold on to your young men
Don't let another man put his plan inside your hand.
Men, hold on to your young ladies
Don't let a man put lies into their head
And drive them crazy.
Men, hold and love your wife
Support her and assure her that you'll be there
For the rest of your life.
Women, love and hold your husband
Kiss him, let him know that he is a good man.
Families, hold on to Christ for the rest of your life
When things go wrong; he'll make them all right.

The Hood

If I have to go to the hood,
Which people consider is no good,
To find my Queen, that would be an unusual thing
I don't want to get the pick of the litter
A lady who's caught on looks, money and everything that glitters
Not a lady that every man is hollering at
Give her conversation, money and she is lying on her back
Give me the one that in school wasn't too cool
Nor a class clown or a girl that always got down
Nor a party girl; man, that's the worst thing in the world
Man, I want a girl after my own heart,
You get a hood girl; she will pull you apart.

How I Love You

Before I met you, I fell in love with you,
How is that? Because I prayed for you,
It may sound kind of crazy; it may sound kind of wrong,
But the feelings I have for you are real and very strong
You are the apple of my eye.
You're so beautiful, smart and I'll never try
To take away what God has blessed me with you on today,
That's how much I love you.

What Do You Want From Me?

Just relax; I'm not here to attack you.
But, I have a question:
I hope you're woman enough to have an answer
What do you want from me?
A puppet on a string?
A relationship that's going up and down?
That will never be.
What happened?
Did a man destroy your mind
saying he'd be there for you always?
Then he left you behind?
You tell your friends you want me to be the man;
Good to you and your kids.
That's something I always did.
When I tried to hug you; you pushed me away.
When I tried to be serious;
all you wanted to do was play.
I'm tired of playing these games,
So I decided to walk away.
You look out your front door, crying;
Saying, "Please don't go, please, please stay".
You slammed the door, then hit the floor.
Then your heart begins to bleed,
But what do you want from me?
You get yourself together and you tell your friends I wasn't the man.
But God blessed me with you and put you into my hands.
Couldn't you see what a blessing I could be?
So, please answer my question,
What do you want from me?

Lead Me

Hold my hand. It's time for you to take command
Lead me, steer me to a place where I need to be
Build me up, but don't throw me in the dumps,
Re-build my heart,
From where many have come, broke me down and tore it apart.
Take my hands;
Teach me how to be more productive with them
And do the best I can.
My face, beautiful but broken,
Thank you for all the encouraging words.
Also, for helping me to stop all that smoking
My arms as powerful as they may be
Help me to realize God blessed me with them,
Not to destroy, but to build unity
My legs; muscular, big and strong
Help me to use them to run to do right
Instead of always ready to run to do wrong.
My mind; it's about that time,
For you to lead me, where I need to be.

2 - Faced

How can you be a pastor of a church
When all you want to do is hurt?
A woman wants counseling, but she wants it alone
Your wife says, "Honey, I'll see you when you get home".
You closed the door 'cause you know she's a whore,
Your pants come down, then all your business hits the town.
How can you be a Deacon of a church?
When all you do is hurt.
We're thinking that you're alright
But looks can be deceiving.
You're clubbing and drinking all through the night.
Your wife calls you on the phone 'cause she doesn't know.
You tell her you're working overnight and you have to go.
How can you be a Mother of the church?
When all you want to do is hurt.
You tell all your friends that your marriage is going to end.
When in fact, you have another man on the side
and you're enjoying the ride.
How can you be a Choir member of a church?
When all you want to do is hurt.
Looking at all the girls, saying you're going to rock their world,
But, do they know that you are gay? That's all I have to say.
How can you be a Member of the church
When all you want to do is hurt?
Now that you're doing everything, do you know all
the disappointment it brings
When you go to church, they don't know all the hurt
They're just looking at the money you bring
It's a sad thing.
Now, the finger is pointed at you,
So what are you going to do?

You Are the One for Me

When I first looked into your eyes,
That's when I realized; you are the one for me.
You're sexy in every way, I must say
I love your walk, the way you talk
The way you glide across the floor.
Who could ask for more?
Nothing can turn me away
From the beauty that's on your face
YOU ARE THE ONE FOR ME!

Choices

Think about the choices you make
They can also be the biggest risks you take.
When you're dropping seeds as you grow
These same seeds will follow wherever you go.
Walking around being nasty and rude
Thinking someone owes you something.
Bad attitude, low esteem,
You know what I mean
When people try to be nice and help you
You think it's a dream.
God blessed you with a nice body and a cute face
Don't get conceited, stuck-up, or arrogant.
You can be replaced.
Choices you make to do wrong or do right;
Those are decisions we struggle with through the night
Remember a choice you make
Could mean the last breath you take.

My Heart Cries

The more I look into the mirror,
Nothing seems any clearer,
Why do I cry from all the pain inside?
When I'm happy, that's when I'm sad.
When I'm upset, that's when I'm glad.
Things are all mixed-up; yet I can't fix them up.
My heart still cries,
Trying to pick up and start all over
The more I try to stand up straight,
The more I bend my shoulders,
Why oh why does my heart still cry?
The more I try to stop the pain, the more I die inside.
I pray every day for the pain to go away
But I can't lie, nor would I deny; the more I pray
The more my heart still cries.

My Friend

I will always love you, my friend.
I will love you to the very end.
Oh how I remember when we talked on the phone
About how our day went and the different things going on,
Playing tricks on one another.
You were my best friend, better than all the others.
I told you my problems every day.
You smiled; encouraging me to have faith, continue to pray.
When I was down, you picked me up.
When you came around, you were my good luck.
You were always there for me, but how could I not see
That deep down inside, you were leaving me?
You cheered me up when I was down,
When I tried to be sad, you said, "Hey, stop wearing that frown".
I remember how we made promises to one another
So we kept the other, we didn't bother
The times we shared were not that rare
To this day, you could never be compared to any other.
You're my friend. I'll love you until the end.

Only God Knows

Only God knows when the world will stop all this mess
Dealing with all kinds of stress.
But I must confess,
It's hard passing this test.
Look at our church world today,
We're smoking, drinking and cursing every day.
When you're living for God; He changes your mind.
Looking for a better future and leaving the past behind,
Looking to God who is the center of our hopes,
Now, let's stop this clubbing, cussing and smoking this dope.
Look around at the destruction in our town
It's not too late to get it straight
So, it's time we give God our heart
Trust him in everything; that's a beginning, a start.
Come on, let's start today,
To pave a better and Godly way.

Heartbreak

Heartbreak; can you relate?
My heart is torn in two because of something you wanted to do
If you weren't ready, you should let me know
Because I ponder in my heart that with you we would always grow
Just another heartbreak
Could it be that I was that surprised?
Of all those tricks you performed before my eyes
The cheating, late night calling, the lies
I came to a conclusion then realized
You never had my best interest at heart
If that was the case, you would not have torn it apart
All the late night running around,
All the stories; I hear that you were out getting down
Look at the heartbreak, heartache
All the things that it's going to take
For me to try to get over the pain
At the moment, on my heart, your name remains
I know in my heart I have to be strong
To look past you, the bitterness and all this wrong
I have to cope but found new hope
But it wasn't in you,
But it was in the man that made me (Jesus) that's true.

Springtime

Springtime is always on my mind
Don't get me wrong, I love the winter time songs,
How we used to warm up by the fireplace
While I was looking at the expression on your face.
Seeing the snow as it flows from the clouds
Kids playing, laughing and talking loud
Then there's the fall; Man! We had a ball
Playing in the grass as we raked the leaves
Being mischievous as we wanted to be
Then the summer; hot, sweat, dripping down my back
Women wearing short, oh so short---enough of that
Playing basketball late into the night
Talking to my girl until the break of dawn's early light
Springtime, it's about a refreshing in the air
Stop, can you smell it, see it, hear it; it's right there.
To heal hurts, repair bad relationship, so don't trip
Springtime is all about starting anew
But it can't do it without you.

Thirsty

I'm thirsty for your word
To tell people of your story, to some that have never heard
Quench my thirst until I want no more,
Overflow my cup until I hit the floor.
Praying and thanking you for paving the way,
So that I could be prosperous and to see another day
Thanking you for the strength to pray for my enemies and friends
Continue to pray for your glory
My thirst for you will never end
Thirsting for you every morning as I cover all the bases
Opening the window, just to see all the faces
Of the thirst you're filling in the world.
You're blessing men, women, boys and girls
So we lift our cups to you, Lord
We thank you for filling them up
So we don't have to thirst any more.

Touch Me

Touch me and see if you can feel
That all the love I have for you is real.
Touch my chest and feel my heart beat.
I get so excited, every time we meet.
When you're around all I want to do is smile
Laugh, act silly and have fun.
When I'm in your arms, I know I am the one.
You bring out the kid in me.
Why can't you see that a touch from you
Does something to me.
I can't talk right, walk right;
I'm up all through the night.
Being around you stirs up my appetite.
When I'm around you my speech is a stutter
I held your hand and I melted like fresh butter.
Don't you know or can't you see?
I need a touch from you
Like you need a touch from me.

Knowledge

If knowledge is the king, then where is its crown?
If the book is the key, then why do we put it down?
Smart, intelligent, easy to relate,
Trying to be better than others,
Exaggerate
We're dying from the lack of
Knowledge
So does that mean I have to go to college?
To read about an American dream
Do you know what I mean?
To understand a plan
Regardless if you're a woman or a man
Knowledge is puffed up by what the Bible says
But can wisdom pave a more excellent way?
So if knowledge is the king
Why don't we use it to do the right thing?

Why do you?

Why do you beat me, kick me, slap me?
Being good to you; that's all I wanted to do.
I cooked you three meals a day.
A simple thank you is a reply I want for you to say.
Why do you do the things you do?
Can't you see the love I have for you is true.
You're out all through the night,
I'm pacing the floor, praying that everything is alright
You come home from the club
You jumped in the bed then you want to rub.
I pushed you away. I don't want to feel that. No, not today.
You get mad then you throw your hand in the air
I jumped out of bed and then I started to stare.
I don't want to fight,
But if I have to it'll be the fight of my life.
But to my surprise, tears started rolling from my eyes.
He screams out, "I apologized."
I can't take this anymore,
I didn't mean to treat you like a whore.
I was told if I mistreat you
If you stay, then your love is true.
I promise, baby, it will never happen again
I'll start treating you as my wife, lover, and my best friend
We looked each other in the eyes
Without telling any lies
He told me that I love you
I held his hand and told him that I love you too.

Eaves Dropping

Excuse me, I overheard your conversation
And I have something to say.
So, be patient with me; don't take it the wrong way.
You said you want a man that's gentle, kind and meek.
Every time there's a party, you're from club to club,
From street to street.
You said you want a good man with money
And who goes to church.
No matter how good that man is, he's not going to deal with you
With all that drama and past hurts.
You're filling his head with lies.
You don't do this and you don't do that.
We all know that you are a Drama Queen and that's a fact.
So, let me give you some helpful advice, if you don't mind.
To get a good man you have to be of the same kind.
All these categories you want in a man,
Make sure you bring the same to the table
Before you take him by the hand.
If he goes to church, then you go too.
Don't be the hypocrite and do the same as they do.
If he has money, then you know the deal.
It's better to have together than to lie, cheat or steal.
Most of all acknowledge God, in all your ways.
When you start praying, you must step out the way.
Now the good man is coming.
Have a blessed day.

Stop

Ladies, this poem is especially for you,
So you can stop doing the things that you do.
Stop, Ladies from cursing yourself
And all that self pity. Tell someone else.
Stop treating these men like spoiled kids
Giving them everything that they want. Yes you did!
Men are staying at home.
They take you to work, then they want to roam,
Driving all over town, running up all the gas
Talking to those young girls and, yes, they are really fast.
Better yet, they're at home, playing video games,
You call him at home, he's disrespecting your name.
Day after day, you're stressing out and your hair's falling out.
You're so mad that you started to fuss.
A co-worker says, "Good morning", then you started to cuss.
Ladies, you got to break this curse.
Instead of getting better, you're getting worse.
You say, "When I first met him, he had a lot of drive".
Now when you get home, to the bed he wants to dive.
You have a big decision to make.
Every Friday you get paid, but your check he takes.
Your mom you asked for money.
When you go over there, you're taking bread, milk, and honey.
The only way you're going to get some rest
Is you have to put that faith to the test.
Kick him and the clothes that he has out.
That will give you something to shout about.
You can do it; make it on your own.
Don't try to call that sorry man on the phone.
Once you take authority over your life and yourself,
Then take the memories of him and put them on the shelf.

Good Bye

How can I say goodbye
Without starting to cry
My heart is saying, "why o' why"
Now it's time for me to survive.
Goodbye to you my friend.
Will I ever see you again?
Looking at those pictures,
Rubbing your face
Remember all those letters
And how no one could take your place.
Thinking about the time we shopped at the mall.
I never laughed so hard until I saw you play basketball.
I cooked for you when you came home from work.
Thank you for accepting my apology when I acted like a jerk.
Mid-day rendezvous,
We stayed out late until the sky changed from light to dark blue.
Walking down the street,
Stopping for a moment while we got something to eat.
Late at night was my delight.
We would watch TV on the couch
And turn the lights off.
Ouch!
It seemed like yesterday that you came my way.
Now you see why it's hard for me to say,
"Goodbye".

Forever

I'll love you forever.
I'll be there for you forever.
No matter what time, day or weather,
I'll be there for you, no matter what you do
Because my love for you will always be true.
On the cross, for you, I gave up my life
So that you might have a right to eternal life.
For you, I call my dearest friend.
My love for you will never end.
So, when I died and tears rolled from your eyes
You'll be in my heart;
It'll never be torn apart.
For I love you forever,
And forever my love will be.

24

Two men met at a park, a little before it got dark.
The older man asked the younger man,
"If you had 24 hours to live, what would you give?"
The young man asked himself, "What would I give?
Let me see. Maybe give some helpful advice
On how I lived my life.
All the wrong and struggles that I had to go through
I pray you don't have to go through the same thing too.
Maybe give my money to help in some type of research
Instead of chasing ladies, trying to get in their skirts.
Do I give away all my material things
To see all the happiness that it brings?"
The young man got into some deep thoughts.
He said,
"I know I'll give my testimony on how I served Jesus Christ
So that you too might have a right to eternal life."
You might only have 24 hours to live
Because every day we're dying.
So, why aren't we trying to get our lives straight
Before 24 hours is over and it's too late?

Yes, Lord

Yes, Lord to your will and to your way.
Several times you tried to warn me, but I didn't obey.
You spared my life
While people around me were getting killed
With a gun or a knife.
My loved ones were dying on every side.
I couldn't go to the funerals, all I could do was cry.
You spared me at the club
When guns came out blazing.
Seven days later, my friend's grave they dug.
I was drinking, driving and smoking dope,
I was trying my best to make it home,
Praying for your grace and mercy and some of my own hope.
Drug dealing was my story;
Trying to make money, buy cars, chasing women
And trying to get some of this world's glory.
I finally got busted and landed in jail.
Man that was the worst thing, like being in hell.
Guards were telling me what to do.
I went to court and someone stole my shoe.
Men were getting raped and the nasty food, boy I did hate.
I was up all night always ready to fight.
I screamed out, "Lord, why is this happening to me?"
He answered, "You didn't want to be free.
The more I asked you to do my will, you lied.
'I'll do it tomorrow', is how you replied".
I repented that night.
It was time for me to get it right.
God blessed me to get out of jail,
Someone I didn't know paid my bail.
Now, I'm preaching the Gospel up and down the street.
That's why I told you my story.
Maybe one day we can meet.

Blood, Sweat & Tears

It was the blood that saved me.
It was the blood that raised me.
The blood that runs through my soul
Is the blood that built me up,
When I'm torn down and scorned.
It was the blood, sweat and tears
That kept me through the years.
When I was in my mother's womb
I was a man whose life would be doomed.
A man child would be raised in the hood
Where there's pimping, drug selling and that's no good.
It took my mother's blood,
sweat and tears to remove me from all my fears.
Just like Christ
Who gave His life
While He was on the cross.
They pierced Him in the side.
He didn't cry nor did He sigh,
But through His blood, sweat and tears,
He's still removing you from all your fears.

Mother

O' how I remember like it was yesterday,
When the death angel came lurking your way.
It was a dark and gloomy day.
When I got the news, I didn't know what to say.
Tears started rolling down my face.
I was trying to find some keys that had previously misplaced.
In my spirit, I felt your pain.
I had to get myself together
Before I could drive through the rain.
As I started out the door,
My knees buckled and I hit the floor.
"God, please, don't take my mother," I pray.
"Let her win the battle and live to see another day".
I jumped into the car and the faster I drove
I felt your pain and how it was tearing your soul.
I see it heart attack after heart attack.
The doctor was operating and she was on her back.
The more I thought about it, the harder I hit the gas,
Wondering how much longer would my mother last.
When I got to the hospital, I was in disarray
To see the expression on my family's face.
Some started crying, others said, "She's dying".
Deep down, I knew they were lying.
God let me know that she was alright;
The death angel came, but he lost this fight.
My mother is back in her same place.
While she was going through her struggles
I saw God's face.
I hope this poem inspires you because it's a true story.
I wanted to share it with you so you too can see God's glory.

Meet the Author

John Mask is originally from Gary, Indiana, the eighth of ten children, and the youngest of three boys. His parents, Floyd Mask Sr. and Darlene Nelson, divorced when he was a child. His father was a steel worker and mother worked as a delivery room technician. His mother had a tough time raising the ten children by herself, but made the best of the situation by ensuring he and his siblings were constantly in church. As a teenager, John played junior high and high school sports at Bailey Junior High and Lee Wallace High School, both in Gary, Indiana. As a young man without strict oversight and guidance he spent a period of his life experiencing the street-life and hanging out with gangs. This lifestyle nearly consumed him, but the Lord had a way of turning him around when his family relocated to Brownsville, Tennessee. John now has three beautiful children, Marquita, Joshua, and Ashante. He spends most of his time preaching the gospel and writing poetry, and now resides in Memphis, Tennessee.

PURCHASE OTHER BOOKS BY JOHN MASK
ONE MAN'S MIND
A COLLECTION OF POEMS

Contact Curry Brother's Marketing and Publishing Group by visiting www.CurryBrothersPublishing.com, or writing to P.O. Box 62314, Colorado Springs, CO 80962, or visiting your favorite local bookstore.